Piney D Press Presents

Two Books –In-One!

Pink Place

&

Blue Blaze!

Written

&

Illustrated

By

Deb Simpson

Note: Graphics used are from the public domain.

Pink Place

Deb Simpson

Copyright 2011
All Rights Reserved

Except as permitted under the
Copyright Act of 1976, or as stated herein,
no part of this publication
may be reproduced or distributed in any form
or by any means or stored in a database
or retrieval system without the prior
written permission of the author.

See Special Notes Below

Special Permissions

Special Permission to reproduce pages of this book for use

by/for educators, and/or in therapeutic work with children

is hereby granted by the author/copyright holder.

Tow-For-One Special Edition
Pink Place 2nd Edition
Blue Blaze 1st Edition

ISBN 978-0-615-48979-7

© Deb Simpson 2011

ABOUT CASA
Court Appointed Special Advocates

Remember looking through your yearbook from sixth grade and seeing the blank space for a boy who wasn't present on "picture day"? Or perhaps you remember the girl in third grade who moved away and missed the class play even though she was supposed to have a part. What about the boy who's name nobody could remember because he only attended your fifth grade class for a month before moving to another school? All too often, this is the legacy of the children who are served by CASA volunteers, or Court Appointed Special Advocates.

The CASA children are caught in the child welfare system because their parents or other caregivers were unprepared to meet their most basic needs. These children have been removed from their homes and placed into the child welfare system where social workers and lawyers and judges with too much work to do have too little time to give to each child.

Every child deserves to find the safety and security of their own "**Pink Place**"; just as each child is entitled to be inspired by the drive of their own "**Blue Blaze**."

Through the efforts of the extraordinary women and men who serve as CASA volunteers, children can have the opportunity to grow up in the loving embrace of a family. These dedicated individuals work through the Juvenile Court system to ensure that every child has the opportunity to be protected and nurtured throughout their childhood. CASA volunteers make certain that their children are safe, that they receive an appropriate education, and that they have a stable adult in their lives who will help them navigate the path from childhood into adulthood.

CASA volunteers believe in the possibilities for all children. Through simple acts of kindness and caring; children are able to develop hope for their future and for their children's future as well.

Susan T. Maguigan

Susan T. Maguigan
Executive Director
CASA of Rutherford County

Support CASA
Through the purchase of this book.
A portion of each retail sale is donated to
CASA of Rutherford County, TN.

To learn more about CASA, or to become a CASA volunteer, see
www.CasaForChildren.org

This book is dedicated to my granddaughter, Samantha

May you find your own special safe place inside your heart and soul.

May this book help each person who reads it to remember that we each have the tools inside of us to survive and thrive!

A VISIT TO PINK PLACE

MAKES EVERYTHING RIGHT

IT MUFFLES THE FEELINGS

OF ANGER & FRIGHT

PINK PLACE IS WONDROUS

HAPPY & BRIGHT

IT'S FILLED WITH **PINK** CLOUDS

& BATHED IN **PINK** LIGHT

IT'S NOT HARD TO GO THERE... ALL IT TAKES IS TO DREAM....

JUST CLOSE YOUR EYES SOFTLY & THINK OF MOONBEAMS ...

IMAGINE
A
PINK
POODLE

A
PINK
PONY

&
PINK
CATS

A CAROUSEL

A FERRIS WHEEL

& A CLOWN IN A PINK HAT

PRETEND A FRIEND IN A CAR THAT'S ALL PINK

SHE'S SHAGGY & WAGGY AND KNOWS WHAT YOU THINK !

WHATEVER YOU NEED SHE ALWAYS CAN FIND

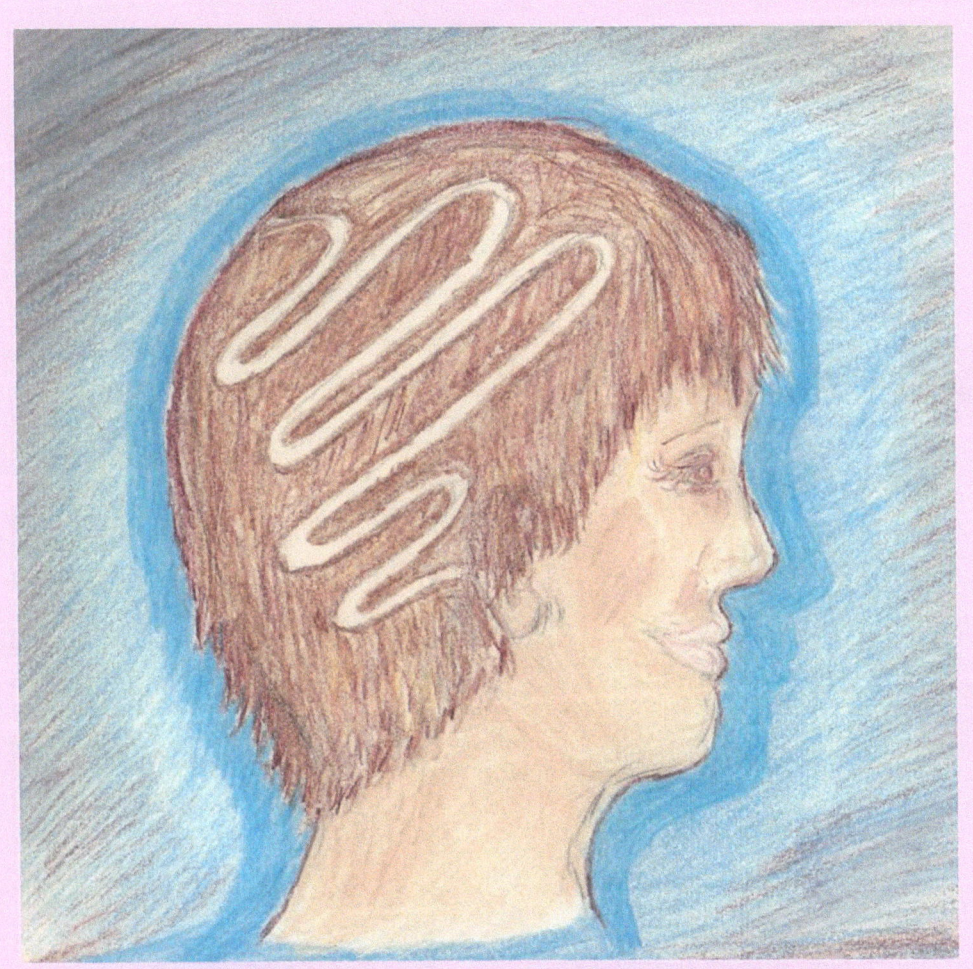

SHE'LL SEARCH HIGH & LOW IN THE TUNNELS OF YOUR MIND

SHE'LL CARRY IT TO YOU AS YOU SIT ON YOUR CLOUD

SHE'LL LAY IT BEFORE YOU AND SAY

LOUD & PROUD

I KNEW YOU HAD IT IN YOU
I KNEW YOU COULD DO IT

IF YOU BELIEVE IN YOURSELF, YOU'LL ALWAYS COME THROUGH IT

THEN YOU AND YOUR FRIEND CAN SLEEP & FEEL SAFE

CUDDLED UP CLOSE INSIDE A PINK CAVE

BUT WHEN THE WORLD SEEMS ALL CLOUDY AND GREY

OR WAVES OF RED ANGER COME CRASHING YOUR WAY

OR EVEN THOSE TIMES WHEN YOU CAN'T FIND YOUR SMILE

JUST GO TO YOUR PINK PLACE & AFTER A WHILE ....

YOU'LL FEEL BETTER!

IT'S A MAGICAL PLACE ONE NO ONE ELSE KNOWS

A PLACE
DEEP INSIDE YOU
WHERE
NO ONE ELSE GOES

IT'S A VERY SPECIAL PLACE
AND IT'S ONLY FOR YOU

BUT YOURS CAN BE PINK....
OR PURPLE OR BLUE....

IT COULD EVEN BE A RAINBOW, IF THAT'S WHAT YOU CHOOSE!

IT'S ALL UP TO YOU!

SO, TURN THE PAGE AND LET'S CREATE

YOUR OWN SPECIAL PLACE

IN YOUR OWN FAVORITE SHADE

SELECT YOUR
1) FAVORITE COLOR (S)
2) FAVORITE ANIMAL FRIEND
3) NAME FOR YOUR SPECIAL PLACE

HERE ARE SOME ANIMAL SKETCHES TO HELP YOU DECIDE AND DRAW:

Turn the Page And Discover Blue Blaze!

Other Books By
Deb Simpson

Pink Place
1st Edition

One Moment
One Memory
One Motion

A memoir

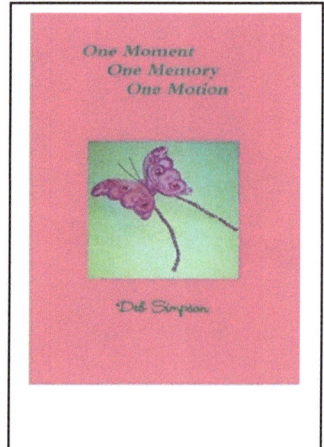

Coming Soon
Closing the Gate
*The biography of Deb's brother,
a former Heaven's Gate Cult member*

THIS BOOK IS DEDICATED TO
MY GRANDSON
NICHOLAS
A LOVER OF CARS
AND ALL THINGS WITH WHEELS!

MAY YOU ALWAYS HAVE THE DESIRE AND
DRIVE TO REACH FOR YOUR DREAMS

BLAZE ON
BLAZE BLUE
REACH FOR THE DRIVE
INSIDE OF YOU!

IT'S A DRIVE DEEP INSIDE A FUEL THAT YOU NEED

TO PUSH YOURSELF FORWARD WITH SPLENDIFEROUS SPEED

LIKE A
TORCH
IN THE
DARK

THAT BEGINS
WITH A SPARK

THIS BLAZE OF BLUE
BEGINS WITH YOU

IMAGINE YOURSELF FLYING WITH A STARSHIP IN SPACE

IMAGINE YOURSELF WINNING A WORLD FAMOUS RACE

IMAGINE YOUR-SELF GLIDING LIKE A KITE WITH NO CARE

IMAGINE YOURSELF FLOATING LIKE A CLOUD ON THE AIR

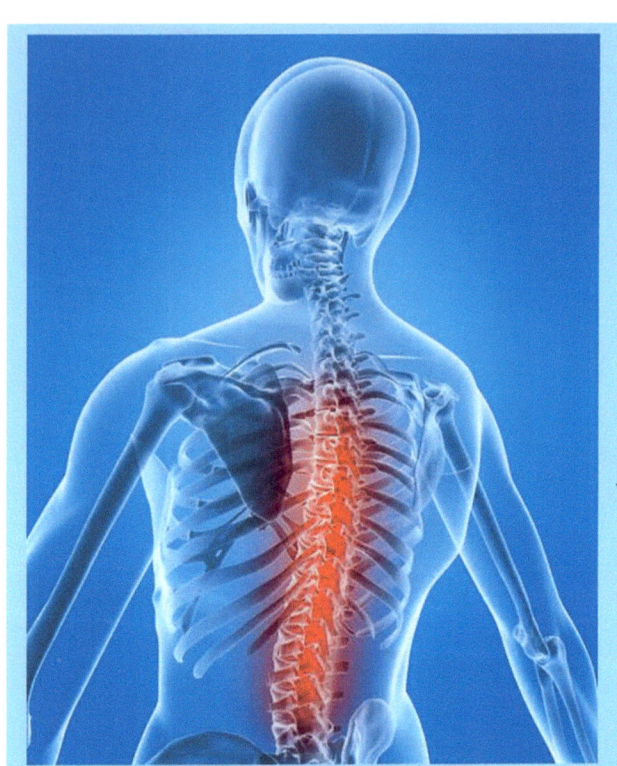

IMAGINE YOU CAN FEEL

STEEL IN YOUR SPINE

IMAGINE YOU CAN SEE
SPARKS IN YOUR MIND

IMAGINE YOU CAN FEEL SPEED IN YOUR WALK

IMAGINE YOU CAN HEAR YOURSELF RAPIDLY TALK

YOU CAN FLY WITHOUT WINGS

SAIL WITHOUT WIND

MOVE AROUND MOUNTAINS

LIKE A TRAIN

Rounds A BEND

YOU CAN SOAR WITH SELF-CONFIDENCE

BLAST PAST THOSE WHO WAIT

CRUSH THE COMPETITION

BE 1ST AT THE GATE!

SO…IF THERE IS SOMETHING

YOU REALLY WANT TO DO ..

SOMETHING THAT'S REALLY IMPORTANT TO YOU

YOU KNOW WHAT YOU NEED

STEEL WHEELS & SPEED

SO-GET STARTED!
LET'S GO!
YOU TAKE THE LEAD!

PICK OUT A COLOR THAT YOU REALLY LIKE

DREAM THE FASTEST-EVER-RACER CAR, TRUCK, OR BIKE

START OFF WITH IT SMALL

WATCH IT GROW T-A-L-L

GIVE IT SOME FLAMES

& A SPLENDIFEROUS NAME

FUEL UP YOUR ENGINE

FEEL YOUR INNER DRIVE

BLUE BLAZE IS INSIDE!

ARE YOU READY TO RIDE?

Blaze On!!

Blaze Blue!

CREATE YOUR OWN BLUE BLAZE

1) PICK THE WHEELS THAT YOU LIKE-CAR, TRUCK, TRAIN, PLANE OR BIKE
2) PICK THE COLOR YOU CHOOSE-IT'S ALL UP TO YOU
3) IMAGINE THE DRIVE FROM DEEP DOWN INSIDE

HERE'S SOME IDEAS
TO START YOUR ENGINE!

Blue Blaze is Born!
A creation from Cliff Cox of Sparta, TN

About Deb Simpson

Deb Simpson writes poetry, fiction and nonfiction.
Her articles and poems have been featured in literary journals,
anthologies, newspapers, online magazines,
and industry publications

Deb lives near Nashville, Tennessee, with her husband,
Paul, and their three cat-kids. She works full time in the
medical products Quality Assurance field, and advocates for the
CASA program for children

Deb's grandmother was one of the strongest influences in her life, and
she hopes to be a similar influence in the lives of her grandchildren
and the children she advocates for
in the CASA program.

Deb's hobbies include reading, writing, sewing, & crochet.

Find Deb on the Web @
Www.DebSimpsonBooks.com
And on Facebook and Twitter!

www.ingramcontent.com/pod-product-compliance
Lightning Source LLC
Chambersburg PA
CBHW060821090426

42738CB00002B/61